PHONICS BINGO!

CONSONANTS & SHORT VOWELS

10 Reproducible Games to Build Key Reading Skills

MICHELLE STURM

Editor: Lynne M. Wilson
Cover design: Cynthia Ng
Interior design: Jaime Lucero
Interior illustrations: Doug Jones, Rob McClurkan, The Noun Project, all other images © Shutterstock.com

ISBN 978-1-5461-0648-7

TABLE OF CONTENTS

Welcome to *Phonics Bingo! Consonants & Short Vowels*

Research shows that children's enthusiasm to learn soars when they engage in purposeful play.[1] That's why *Phonics Bingo! Consonants & Short Vowels* is a great way to help kids master letter sounds. This academic twist on the classic bingo game helps lay a strong phonics foundation for early readers. Once that groundwork is developed, children will be able to focus on meaning and comprehension instead of decoding and mechanics, putting them on the path to becoming lifelong learners.

The Science of Reading is an ever-growing body of research that combines neurological, psychological, and cognitive science findings about how we learn to read. Phonics experts and reading researchers emphasize the importance of explicit sound-spelling instruction accompanied by ample opportunities for practice. According to author and phonics specialist Wiley Blevins, "Fluency is critical and … is an outcome of constant review and repetition using sound-spelling knowledge to blend words in context."[2] *Phonics Bingo! Consonants & Short Vowels* provides an engaging and effective way to weave that review and repetition into your literacy program. With each game they play, children will strengthen their new phonics skills.

---

[1] Allee-Herndon, Karyn and Killingsworth Roberts, Sherron. "The Power of Purposeful Play in Primary Grades: Adjusting Pedagogy for Children's Needs and Academic Gains." *Journal of Education*, vol. 201, issue 1, 2020, pp. 54-63, journals.sagepub.com/doi/10.1177/0022057420903272 2020. Accessed 3 May 2023.
[2] Blevins, Wiley. *Phonics From A to Z: A Practical Guide*, 4th ed. Scholastic Inc. 2023.

Children benefit from a phonics sequence that prioritizes higher-frequency sound-spelling relationships and intricacy of sound-spellings. Many reading specialists suggest sequencing letter sounds by both their complexity and their frequency of use, rather than following traditional alphabetical order. In *Phonics Bingo! Consonants & Short Vowels*, you'll find 10 game sets, each made up of 24 caller's cards and eight reproducible game boards, that follow that guidance. The first five game sets target initial consonant sounds. The next two sets focus on final consonant sounds, and the remaining three sets cover short vowels in CVC words. This progression guides children through essential phonics milestones in a targeted sequence.

There are various ways to incorporate *Phonics Bingo! Consonants & Short Vowels* into your instruction. For example, children can play in small groups or as a whole class. A whole-class structure works well when reviewing or reinforcing specific sound-spelling relationships. However, if you are introducing a new letter sound, starting with small groups allows for a more focused lesson. Initially you may want to lead game rounds, using the "How to Play" instructions on the next page. Once children are familiar with the rules and boards, you can place the bingo games in learning centers. With this more independent approach, children can take turns as the "Caller" and play with minimal adult support.

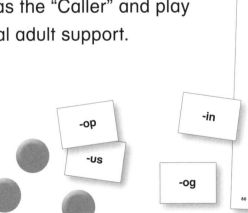

How to Play

1. Using the table of contents, find the set that supports your target skill(s).

2. Make copies of the bingo boards and caller's cards.

3. Cut apart the caller's cards. Shuffle the cards and stack them upside down.

4. Give each player a board and tokens or counters.

5. Preview the illustrations on the boards to ensure that players know what each picture represents.

6. Draw the top card from your caller's card stack and read aloud the letter sound on the card. Set the called cards aside so you can verify any winning bingo boards.

7. After a card is read, have players check their boards to see if they have a match for the target sound or word. Any player who finds a match should place a token on the matching space. (Alternatively, you might choose to have children color matches they find on their boards.) *Only one match can be made per turn.*

8. When a player gets four matches in a row vertically, horizontally, or diagonally, the player should call out, "Bingo!"

9. Any player who calls out must then correctly read the word on each covered space to win the game. Note: Multiple winners are possible.

Beginning Consonants *m, p, s, t*   Caller's Cards

Cut out the cards. Shuffle and place them in a stack. Pull the top card and read the sound. You might say: *The sound is /m/ as in* mouse. *If you have a word on your board that starts with the /m/ sound, cover that square. If you have more than one match, cover only* **one**.

/m/	/p/	/s/	/t/
/m/	/p/	/s/	/t/
/m/	/p/	/s/	/t/
/m/	/p/	/s/	/t/
/m/	/p/	/s/	/t/
/m/	/p/	/s/	/t/

Beginning Consonants *m, p, s, t*

pear	panda	turtle	sun
tent	piano	saw	mop
mitten	money	pan	popcorn
table	moon	pizza	seal

Beginning Consonants *m, p, s, t*

pencil	toe	monkey	mask
socks	maze	paint	turkey
mountain	tape	pancakes	mouse
sun	milk	tent	pirate

Beginning Consonants *m, p, s, t* ③

pumpkin	saw	ten	socks
table	seal	moon	mitten
turtle	tiger	money	panda
popcorn	pear	mask	mountain

Beginning Consonants *m, p, s, t*　(4)

seal	pizza	saw	monkey
milk	ten	pan	paint
popcorn	tail	pirate	table
map	pin	sun	sandals

Beginning Consonants *m, p, s, t*

salt	pumpkin	maze	pear
ten	saw	toe	popcorn
turkey	money	mask	pizza
moon	table	pan	mountain

Beginning Consonants *m, p, s, t*

6

pan	mask	saw	seal
monkey	popcorn	milk	toe
tent	mitten	panda	paint
socks	pencil	mountain	tiger

Beginning Consonants *m, p, s, t*

7

piano	turkey	popcorn	toe
money	mountain	tail	moon
salt	tent	seal	pancakes
sun	mouse	milk	pirate

Beginning Consonants *m, p, s, t* (8)

turtle	tent	mitten	pan
seal	maze	socks	paint
mask	pumpkin	pizza	sandals
moon	map	tiger	tape

Beginning Consonants *c, d, n, r*   Caller's Cards

Cut out the cards. Shuffle and place them in a stack. Pull the top card and read the sound. You might say: *The sound is* /n/ *as in* neck. *If you have a word on your board that starts with the* /n/ *sound, cover that square. If you have more than one match, cover only* **one.** *Note: In this set, the letter* c *stands for the* /k/ sound, as in *cat.*

/k/	/d/	/n/	/r/
/k/	/d/	/n/	/r/
/k/	/d/	/n/	/r/
/k/	/d/	/n/	/r/
/k/	/d/	/n/	/r/
/k/	/d/	/n/	/r/

Beginning Consonants *c, d, n, r*   ① 1

neck	dog	can	duck
needle	deer	candle	corn
nine	dive	carrot	rabbit
nest	car	cap	rain

Beginning Consonants c, d, n, r

2

nose	dinosaur	castle	ring
nail	door	cane	rain
neck	cow	cat	rocket
needle	car	camel	robot

Beginning Consonants *c, d, n, r*   ③

net	dice	ruler	rug
nine	dive	rabbit	rain
dinosaur	can	duck	candle
nest	cane	robot	rocket

Beginning Consonants *c, d, n, r*

4

duck	nose	car	ring
needle	deer	cat	corn
nine	dive	carrot	rabbit
nest	door	cap	rain

Beginning Consonants *c, d, n, r* **5**

dinosaur	neck	cat	rug
nail	duck	cane	ring
net	dice	car	rain
needle	cow	rocket	robot

Beginning Consonants *c, d, n, r*   6

dive	rabbit	ring	rug
cat	camel	nine	rope
rock	castle	cap	duck
robot	deer	nest	cane

Beginning Consonants *c, d, n, r* (7)

dog	rain	candle	ruler
duck	corn	nest	can
carrot	nine	needle	ring
deer	rocket	neck	rock

Beginning Consonants *c, d, n, r*

car	nail	robot	rabbit
ring	rope	rain	net
castle	dog	camel	duck
dinosaur	cat	cane	rug

Beginning Consonants *b, f, h, l* Caller's Cards

Cut out the cards. Shuffle and place them in a stack. Pull the top card and read the sound. You might say: *The sound is* /b/ *as in* ball. *If you have a word on your board that starts with the* /b/ *sound, cover that square. If you have more than one match, cover only* **one**.

/b/	/f/	/h/	/l/
/b/	/f/	/h/	/l/
/b/	/f/	/h/	/l/
/b/	/f/	/h/	/l/
/b/	/f/	/h/	/l/
/b/	/f/	/h/	/l/

Beginning Consonants *b, f, h, l*

ball	bed	hook	leaf
fence	leg	hanger	light
log	fan	finger	bear
fish	five	feather	lion

Beginning Consonants *b, f, h, l* 2

ladder	balloon	four	bat
lamp	leaf	horse	fire
leg	hand	lock	hose
lemon	bee	book	feather

Beginning Consonants *b, f, h, l*

bell	ladder	harp	bird
lion	box	fence	baby
light	log	heart	horse
lizard	lock	fork	hat

Beginning Consonants *b, f, h, l*

4

house	leg	finger	lemon
hook	balloon	five	bird
hat	box	fire	butterfly
hand	lamp	light	fish

Beginning Consonants *b, f, h, l* 5

hook	ball	finger	lion
fence	bed	ladybug	hanger
lobster	bell	harp	bird
fish	hat	baby	house

Beginning Consonants *b, f, h, l*

bat	lion	lock	lamp
balloon	horse	hook	finger
butterfly	hose	house	bell
bear	lobster	ladder	bed

Beginning Consonants *b, f, h, l*   7

book	lion	leg	balloon
bird	fence	hook	house
feather	lock	hat	lizard
finger	ball	five	lamp

Beginning Consonants *b, f, h, l*   (8)

bee	lock	bird	heart
four	harp	bat	house
fork	hanger	horse	fire
feather	bell	lizard	log

Beginning Consonants *g, j, k, w*   Caller's Cards

Cut out the cards. Shuffle and place them in a stack. Pull the top card and read the sound. You might say: *The sound is /g/ as in* goat. *If you have a word on your card that starts with the /g/ sound, cover that square. If you have more than one match, cover only* **one**. *Note: In this set, the letter *g* stands for the hard /g/ sound.

/g/	/j/	/k/	/w/
/g/	/j/	/k/	/w/
/g/	/j/	/k/	/w/
/g/	/j/	/k/	/w/
/g/	/j/	/k/	/w/
/g/	/j/	/k/	/w/

Beginning Consonants g, j, k, w
1

kangaroo	juice	guitar	king
kite	goose	gorilla	wand
game	worm	wolf	gate
jacket	key	wing	goat

Beginning Consonants *g, j, k, w*

2

jellyfish	gate	wave	karate
jar	wand	watermelon	kitten
key	golf	jet	game
juggle	window	wagon	web

Beginning Consonants *g, j, k, w* (3)

kite	juice	game	golf
jacket	karate	jet	juggle
kangaroo	goose	worm	well
guitar	gorilla	wolf	watch

Beginning Consonants *g, j, k, w*   4

key	jellyfish	window	wagon
jar	watermelon	web	gate
koala	goat	wing	kitten
king	gift	golf	wave

Beginning Consonants *g, j, k, w*

5

juice	jacket	kangaroo	wolf
kite	koala	jar	juggle
game	watermelon	key	wing
guitar	goat	well	wave

Beginning Consonants *g, j, k, w*

wand	karate	gate	web
jellyfish	king	gift	wagon
goose	worm	jacket	goat
gorilla	kitten	window	juggle

Beginning Consonants *g, j, k, w*

7

karate	kangaroo	web	watch
worm	gate	gift	wave
guitar	wing	goat	key
goose	jar	kite	juggle

Beginning Consonants *g, j, k, w* ⑧

jacket	watermelon	kitten	wing
juice	gate	koala	well
game	jet	gorilla	window
jellyfish	king	wagon	wand

Beginning Consonants *q, v, y, z*   Caller's Cards

Cut out the cards. Shuffle and place them in a stack. Pull the top card and read the sound. You might say: The sound is /v/ as in vet. *If you have a word on your card that starts with the /v/ sound, cover that square. If you have more than one match, cover only* **one**. *Note: The letter* q *is usually followed by the letter* u. *Together they stand for the* /kw/ *sound, as in* queen.

/kw/	/v/	/y/	/z/
/kw/	/v/	/y/	/z/
/kw/	/v/	/y/	/z/
/kw/	/v/	/y/	/z/
/kw/	/v/	/y/	/z/
/kw/	/v/	/y/	/z/

Beginning Consonants *q, v, y, z*

1

queen	vase	violin	yarn
zigzag	zipper	vacuum	yolk
yogurt	vest	volcano	zebra
zero	yawn	question	vote

Beginning Consonants *q, v, y, z* ②

yogurt	vest	zipper	yarn
zebra	vase	quiet	volcano
queen	yawn	van	question
yolk	vacuum	vet	quarter

Beginning Consonants *q, v, y, z*

③

vacuum	yarn	zigzag	zebra
queen	zipper	vet	question
yo-yo	volcano	vase	vine
yogurt	vote	quarter	yolk

Beginning Consonants *q*, *v*, *y*, *z*

4

quiet	zigzag	van	vase
yolk	volcano	zipper	yo-yo
queen	yawn	vet	zero
yogurt	vine	quarter	zebra

Beginning Consonants *q, v, y, z*

zigzag	vet	vacuum	yogurt
yarn	vest	van	zipper
zebra	yolk	quarter	violin
queen	yawn	question	volcano

Beginning Consonants *q*, *v*, *y*, *z*

vet	yogurt	question	zipper
yarn	van	zebra	volcano
queen	vacuum	yawn	violin
yolk	vase	zigzag	zero

Beginning Consonants *q, v, y, z*

question	vest	yarn	zigzag
vase	yo-yo	vacuum	zero
zebra	queen	vote	vine
zipper	volcano	yolk	quiet

Beginning Consonants *q, v, y, z* (8)

yawn	yogurt	quarter	quiet
yarn	zero	yolk	question
zipper	van	vet	queen
vase	vote	zebra	zigzag

Ending Consonants *k, l, p, t* Caller's Cards

Cut out the cards. Shuffle and place them in a stack. Pull the top card and read the sound. You might say: *The sound is /l/ as in the end of the word seal. If you have a word on your card that ends with the /l/ sound, cover that square. If you have more than one match, cover only* **one**.

/k/	/l/	/p/	/t/
/k/	/l/	/p/	/t/
/k/	/l/	/p/	/t/
/k/	/l/	/p/	/t/
/k/	/l/	/p/	/t/
/k/	/l/	/p/	/t/

Ending Consonants *k, l, p, t* ①

seal	rock	camel	goat
duck	cup	eight	jet
soap	dot	hip	clock
book	bat	sail	hook

Ending Consonants *k, l, p, t*

nail	beak	well	hat
up	back	yell	dip
feet	nut	mop	cat
chick	sit	ball	dot

Ending Consonants *k, l, p, t*

(3)

check	yell	chick	back
hop	mop	well	clock
nail	feet	rock	dot
cup	bat	cook	ball

Ending Consonants *k, l, p, t*

4

hip	sail	duck	dot
rip	cup	clock	rock
soap	book	jet	ball
hat	well	sick	hook

Ending Consonants *k, l, p, t*

sick	up	eight	sit
seal	beak	clock	heel
kick	goat	bat	net
yell	rip	cup	well

Ending Consonants *k, l, p, t*

pup	soap	rock	hook
nail	dip	hip	feet
duck	eight	jet	clock
bat	well	sick	ball

Ending Consonants *k, l, p, t*

bat	seal	hop	cook
soap	book	nail	goat
duck	nut	hook	sail
hat	rock	dot	up

Ending Consonants *k, l, p, t*

(8)

soap	hook	cup	rip
book	bat	eight	nail
chick	goat	hat	back
up	cook	hop	ball

Ending Consonants *d, g, n, x*   Caller's Cards

Cut out the cards. Shuffle and place them in a stack. Pull the top card and read the sound. You might say: *The sound is* /n/ *as in the end of the word* sun. *If you have a word on your card that ends with the* /n/ *sound, cover that square. If you have more than one match, cover only* **one**. *Note: In this set, the letter *x* stands for the /ks/ sound, as in *fox*.

/d/	/g/	/n/	/ks/
/d/	/g/	/n/	/ks/
/d/	/g/	/n/	/ks/
/d/	/g/	/n/	/ks/
/d/	/g/	/n/	/ks/
/d/	/g/	/n/	/ks/

Ending Consonants *d, g, n, x*

sun	mitten	fox	jug
box	man	pumpkin	wig
bag	cloud	wagon	bird
ax	big	mug	fin

Ending Consonants *d, g, n, x* (2)

box	toad	bed	bug
bird	moon	lion	fox
pen	jug	mad	can
van	fan	six	mix

Ending Consonants *d, g, n, x*

leg	lid	bag	sun
read	balloon	big	men
log	ten	fix	ax
kid	rain	sad	ox

Ending Consonants *d, g, n, x*

4

jug	men	tag	mix
pin	bug	mug	lemon
win	mad	read	sun
ox	six	bed	toad

Ending Consonants *d, g, n, x*

5

wig	ox	leg	sun
mitten	road	can	fin
bag	big	lemon	mix
pin	fix	bird	bed

Ending Consonants *d, g, n, x*

6

bag	mug	sad	can
road	lion	lid	sun
men	bird	mix	lemon
win	ox	bed	jug

Ending Consonants *d, g, n, x*

bug	box	mad	kid
pumpkin	van	wagon	read
bird	ox	road	lemon
balloon	fox	bed	hen

Ending Consonants *d, g, n, x*

kid	cloud	lion	wig
six	man	lid	sun
can	read	mix	lemon
fin	ox	mug	bug

Short Vowels *a, e, u*   Caller's Cards

Cut out the cards. Shuffle and place them in a stack. Pull the top card and read the sound. You might say: *If you have a word on your board that ends with* -at, *as in the end of the word* cat, *cover that square. If you have more than one match, cover only* **one**.

-ag	-ag	-an	-an
-an	-ap	-at	-at
-at	-at	-ed	-eg
-en	-en	-en	-en
-et	-et	-ub	-ug
-us	-ut	-ut	-un

Short Vowels *a, e, u* ⑴

tub	bug	leg	cut
van	hen	vet	tag
jet	nut	hat	bat
sun	bed	ten	men

Short Vowels *a, e, u*

2

map	pan	hen	jet
tub	bed	bug	hat
vet	cat	bus	bag
ten	leg	rat	sun

Short Vowels *a, e, u*

3

pan	van	tub	cat
bus	bed	fan	map
jet	ten	pen	leg
mug	hat	men	rat

Short Vowels *a, e, u*

4

pen	map	leg	cat
ten	van	bus	hat
bed	tub	rat	fan
bug	pan	hen	jet

Short Vowels *a, e, u*

5

ten	pan	jet	bus
bed	bug	van	hat
tub	map	pen	rat
men	cut	fan	cat

Short Vowels *a, e, u*

bed	map	tub	hen
van	mug	pen	ten
cut	jet	bus	hat
cat	rat	fan	pan

Short Vowels *a, e, u*

vet	pan	map	bus
leg	hat	mug	pen
ten	jet	bed	van
cat	fan	tub	rat

Short Vowels *a, e, u*

8

hen	tub	bug	map
van	cut	ten	jet
bed	bag	pen	bus
cat	hat	rat	fan

Short Vowels *i, o, u*   Caller's Cards

Cut out the cards. Shuffle and place them in a stack. Pull the top card and read the sound. You might say: *If you have a word on your board that ends with -it, as in the end of the word* sit, *cover that square. If you have more than one match, cover only* **one**.

-id	-ig	-in	-in
-ip	-ip	-it	-ix
-og	-og	-om	-op
-op	-op	-ot	-ot
-ox	-ox	-ub	-ug
-un	-up	-us	-ut

Short Vowels *i, o, u*

1

box	dog	pot	sit
bug	fox	mop	top
hip	run	rip	cup
bus	fin	kid	pin

Short Vowels *i, o, u*

dog	six	mop	hot
run	pin	pop	mom
bug	hop	dip	cup
box	nut	log	bus

Short Vowels *i, o, u*

3

bug	bus	log	pot
nut	fin	hip	run
box	hop	cup	kid
dog	mop	pop	sit

Short Vowels *i, o, u*

4

fox	hop	run	mom
bug	dog	mop	hot
six	log	pin	top
bus	rip	kit	pup

Short Vowels *i, o, u*

dip	bug	fin	mop
dog	hip	log	pop
box	kid	kit	tub
pin	pot	mom	run

Short Vowels *i, o, u*

6

run	dog	mop	sit
fox	bug	pin	kid
six	log	hot	cup
hop	pop	mom	wig

Short Vowels *i, o, u*

log	fin	bug	top
box	dog	hot	pup
nut	hip	run	kit
mop	pin	pop	zip

Short Vowels *i, o, u* (8)

fin	nut	pin	mop
fox	tub	rip	top
kid	dog	six	mom
log	wig	box	hip

Short Vowels *a, e, o*   Caller's Cards

Cut out the cards. Shuffle and place them in a stack. Pull the top card and read the sound. You might say: *If you have a word on your board that ends with* -an, *as in the end of the word* van, *cover that square. If you have more than one match, cover only* **one**.

-ad	-ag	-an	-an
-ap	-at	-at	-at
-eb	-ed	-eg	-em
-en	-en	-et	-et
-ob	-og	-og	-op
-op	-ot	-ot	-ox

Short Vowels *a, e, o*   1

pot	hat	net	hot
ten	bag	vet	web
sad	dog	map	hop
cat	cob	gem	bat

Short Vowels *a, e, o*

2

bed	mop	fan	men
hat	van	web	leg
box	cat	dog	log
sad	dot	bat	net

Short Vowels *a, e, o*

3

bat

pot

van

web

gem

dog

map

dot

cob

hat

sad

bed

cat

hop

bag

vet

Short Vowels *a, e, o* ④

fan	web	van	sad
ten	vet	hen	bed
mop	cat	fox	leg
log	hat	net	dot

Short Vowels *a, e, o*

leg	dog	map	van
vet	men	pot	gem
cat	bat	ten	cob
hop	bed	hat	pet

Short Vowels *a, e, o*　　6

hen	vet	van	web
cob	cat	dot	fan
hop	log	bat	fox
net	bed	ten	map

Short Vowels *a, e, o*

van	map	fan	bat
log	hen	dot	box
cob	cat	ten	mop
vet	pot	bag	bed

Short Vowels *a, e, o*   8

dog	leg	web	van
bed	cob	men	gem
hat	cat	ten	pot
vet	bag	pet	bat